October [illegible]

25 Questions

About the Pope

Les Miller

NOVALIS

Cover design: Mardigrafe

Cover illustration: Audrey Wells

Interior photographs: iStock: pp. 17, 27; Photographic Service, *L'Osservatore Romano*, p. 15; WP Wittman Photography, pp. 13, 33, 38.

Layout: Mardigrafe and Audrey Wells

Reviewed by Msgr. Dennis Murphy, founder of the Institute for Catholic Education.

Published by Novalis

Publishing Office
10 Lower Spadina Avenue, Suite 400
Toronto, Ontario, Canada
M5V 2Z2

Head Office
4475 Frontenac Street
Montréal, Québec, Canada
H2H 2S2

www.novalis.ca

Library and Archives Canada Cataloguing in Publication

Miller, Leslie, 1952-
25 questions about the Pope / Les Miller.

ISBN 978-2-89646-237-7

1. Papacy--Miscellanea. 2. Popes--Miscellanea.
I. Title. II. Title: Twenty-five questions about the Pope.

BX1805.M54 2010 262'.13 C2010-905359-1

Printed in Canada.

We acknowledge the financial support of the Government of Canada through the Book Publishing Industry Development Program (BPIDP) for our publishing activities.

5 4 3 2 1 15 14 13 12 11

TABLE OF CONTENTS

A Word from the Author

We have all seen pictures of the pope. He often looks like he stepped from the pages of history into our world. In many ways that is who the pope is: a bridge between our tradition and the present day, carrying the message of Christ to a modern world. The pope lives in Vatican City, an independent state in the centre of the city of Rome, Italy. When he can, he travels around the world to visit various countries and their people. While many love the pope, others do not understand his role and his teachings. It is my hope that you will come to know and understand better the important role the pope plays in Catholicism today.

Using a question-and-answer format, we will explore together questions that young people often ask about the pope and the papacy (the office of the pope). This is only the beginning of your search to learn about the pope. For more information, ask your parents, your teacher or catechist, and your parish priest. Check out the many online resources, including the Vatican website (www.vatican.va), the Vatican YouTube channel (www.youtube.com/user/vatican) and the pope's own Facebook page (www.pope2you.net/). May God bless you as you learn more about the pope!

1

Who is the pope?

The pope is the leader of the Roman Catholic Church. He lives in Vatican City, which is a tiny country within the City of Rome. Do you ever have to watch over a younger brother or sister, or a pet? Well, the pope, together with his brother bishops, watches over more than one billion Catholics. Talk about responsibility!

Let's start by looking at a few of the official titles for the pope:

Bishop of Rome: This title goes back to the time of the *apostles*, when the Christians of Rome were led by a person they called *bishop*. This leader is thought to be St. Peter, who was one of Jesus' followers. Peter became the first leader of the early Christians after Jesus died. We call Peter the first pope.

Vicar of Jesus Christ: Vicars were Roman officials who represented the emperor to the people and the people to the emperor. The early Church used this model to describe the special role of the pope. (All bishops are called vicars of Christ, because they succeeded the apostles.)

Successor of the Prince of the Apostles: St. Peter is described as the Prince of the Apostles. The pope is always seen as someone who followed (or succeeded) St. Peter in this job as leader of Christians.

Supreme Pontiff of the Universal Church: In pagan times, the chief priest of Rome (often the Emperor) was given this title. After the Roman Empire became Christian, the title was given to the pope.

Primate of Italy: A *Primate* is the leading bishop in a country. So the pope is the head of the Italian Catholic Church.

Sovereign of the State of Vatican City: The pope is the ruler of a tiny country of 44 hectares (about 100 football fields) called Vatican City.

Servant of the Servants of God: This title goes back 1 500 years, to the days of Pope Gregory I. It was an attempt to show that despite all the other glorious titles given to the pope, the person occupying the office needs to have great humility because he is a servant of the people.

According to the *Catholic Encyclopedia*, there have been 263 popes from St. Peter to Pope Benedict XVI.

Some popes have the same name. We can tell them apart by the Roman numerals after their name. The earlier the pope lived, the lower the numeral. Here are some examples of Roman numerals:

I = 1	VII = 7	XIII = 13	XIX = 19	XXV = 25
II = 2	VIII = 8	XIV = 14	XX = 20	L = 50
III = 3	IX = 9	XV = 15	XXI = 21	C = 100
IV = 4	X = 10	XVI = 16	XXII = 22	D = 500
V = 5	XI = 11	XVII = 17	XXIII = 23	M = 1000
VI = 6	XII = 12	XVIII = 18	XXIV = 24	

Try to figure out what your year of birth looks like in Roman numerals. I was born in 1952, so mine is MCMLII. Hint: a smaller number placed before a bigger number (CM) means you subtract C (100) from M (1000) to get 900.

Since 1958, there have been five popes:

- Blessed John XXIII (1958–63)
- Paul VI (1963–78)
- John Paul I (1978)
- John Paul II (1978–2005)
- Benedict XVI (elected in 2005)

Ask your grandparents or parish priest what they remember about the popes who were in office before you were born.

2

Who was the first pope?

Do you remember the story of Jesus calling the fishermen from their nets to follow him? (You can find it in the Bible: see the Gospel of Matthew [4:18-20] or the Gospel of Mark [1:16-18].) One of these fishermen was Simon, whose name Jesus later changed to Peter. Peter comes from *petros*, the Latin word for "rock." (*Pierre*, Peter's name in French, also means "rock.") Jesus pointed to Simon Peter and said that upon this rock he would build his Church. Peter was a surprising choice. He sometimes didn't understand the teachings or actions of Jesus, he denied knowing Jesus before the crucifixion, and he probably could not read or write. But Jesus chose well: Peter was the first leader of an organization that has lasted for 2 000 years and has more than one billion members.

After the death and resurrection of Jesus, Peter and the other *apostles* spread the Good News of Jesus through the neighbouring countries. When they settled in a new city or town, a *bishop* became their leader. Christians set up a community in Rome, the capital of a huge and powerful empire. Rome was a dangerous place for Christians, because the Roman rulers had outlawed many religions. Many Christians died terrible deaths because of their faith. Some were even used as human targets or as bait in the violent games played in the Roman circuses and tournaments.

Peter quickly ran into trouble with the Roman leaders. He was arrested and then condemned to die. Romans used crucifixion to torture, humiliate and kill their enemies. Peter was seen as an enemy because he was spreading a religion that was different from the Roman religion. Legend has it that Peter told his captors that he did not deserve to die in the same position as Jesus, and so asked to be crucified upside down.

Peter would not have recognized the title "pope," because it wasn't used at that time. It would be a few centuries before the leader of the Church became known as pope. Still, Peter is considered to be the first Bishop of Rome. Rome became the most influential Church community of all for many Christians. Whoever was the Bishop of Rome was seen as the primary leader of the Church.

- It is believed that St. Peter's Basilica, the huge church in Vatican City, was built on the tomb of Peter.
- St. Peter's Basilica can hold 60,000 people, more than any other Christian church in the world. For a virtual tour of this beautiful church, visit http://saintpetersbasilica.org. Millions of people visit the Basilica every year.
- Many early Christians hid from the Roman authorities in underground caverns in Rome called *catacombs*. You can still visit them today.

3

Are popes powerful?

There are different types of power. If you have political power, you can make a difference in how cities and countries treat each other. If you have spiritual power, you can make a difference in people's relationship with God. Let's look at two early popes who had both political and spiritual power.

Leo the Great was pope during the fifth century, when the Roman Empire was crumbling. Warlords such as Attila the Hun destroyed villages and towns as they advanced on Rome. Leo confronted Attila and persuaded him to stop his invasion. At the time, the chaotic political system caused many people to feel unsafe. Leo saw the need for the pope to have a central role, with bishops throughout Western Christianity working with him. Until this time, many bishops were fairly independent, meeting only from time to time to decide important issues. Pope Leo stepped up as a political leader to make places safe so that people could live in peace.

Picture a *monastery*. Close your eyes and imagine monks chanting a beautiful melody. In the year 590, a monk was summoned from his monastery to become Pope Gregory the Great. This intelligent and good man continued the work of Pope Leo the Great in making sure that the Church stayed united and organized, and used political power to keep believers safe. He thought that more people should hear the message of Jesus, so he sent out missionaries to northern Europe, including England. In this way, Pope Gregory used his political power to help spread the message of Jesus.

4

Why do many people expect Pope John Paul II to be named a saint?

When Pope John Paul II died in 2005, many people called on the Church to officially recognize him as a saint. A saint is a person who has lived according to the teachings of Jesus through acts of great devotion, love and service. For many people, Pope John Paul II certainly seems to be one of our saints.

Karol (Polish for "Charles") Wojtyla (pronounced Voy-TEE-wah) was born in Poland in 1920. During the Second World War, he was forced to leave his university studies to serve the Nazi occupiers as a forced labourer in a rock quarry. He secretly joined a group of young people training to be priests. Karol showed great courage by helping others in times of danger and difficulty.

Soon after he became a priest, the Polish Church saw that he would be an intelligent and wise leader. He became a bishop at the young age of 38 and played an important role in the *Second Vatican Council*. Soon after, he was appointed *cardinal*. In 1978, Cardinal Albino Luciani (Pope John Paul I) was elected pope, but died after only 33 days in office. In the election that followed, Cardinal Karol Wojtyla was named pope. He chose Pope John Paul II as his name.

During his reign, he reached out to many groups, including young people, other Christians and other religions. He built these relationships through tireless travel to many countries. Although he carried on many reforms of the Second Vatican Council, he spoke out firmly about some traditional Catholic teachings. For example, he took a strong stand against abortion. He was also an important force in standing up to oppressive communist rule in his home country of Poland and other Eastern European states. He is seen to be one of the most influential people in bringing about the end of communism.

The pope had many enemies because of his strong stands on important issues. In 1981, a man shot and nearly killed him. In one of the most moving scenes in modern times, Pope John Paul II visited the cell of his would-be assassin and forgave him.

In later years, an increasingly frail pope spoke out against some of the worst features of our modern world: violence, greed and a lack of respect for human dignity. Pope John Paul II will long be remembered for reminding the world of the love of Christ.

- John Paul II was pope for 26 years – the second-longest rule in Church history. Pope Pius IX served for 31 years in the 1800s.
- John Paul II was the first Polish pope and the first non-Italian pope since 1522!
- During his pontificate, Pope John Paul II travelled to 129 different countries.

5

Who is Pope Benedict XVI?

After Pope John Paul II died in 2005, Cardinal Josef Ratzinger was elected pope. As a teen growing up in wartime Germany, he joined the Nazi youth, because all boys his age were expected to do so. After the war, Josef became a priest. He was an important advisor at the *Second Vatican Council*. He was later chosen as *Archbishop* and Cardinal of Munich.

Cardinal Ratzinger became Pope John Paul II's most important advisor during his long reign. It was no surprise when other cardinals elected him pope in April 2005.

In the years since his election, Pope Benedict XVI has continued the work of Pope John Paul II in his travels and in his writings. Pope Benedict is seen as a great thinker, but he is a humble, prayerful man who has warmly reached out to youth, the poor and the victimized.

Pope Benedict XVI (78 years old) was 20 years older than Pope John Paul II (58 years old) when elected.

6

How do popes help the world?

The leader of the largest religious group in the world has great responsibility. It is not surprising, then, that many world leaders meet with the pope about matters of global importance.

Beyond offering wise advice, the pope encourages groups in the Church that work to help the poor, the sick and the outcast. The Church supports schools, hospitals, orphanages, homes for people with disabilities, and numerous charities.

The Church is also working to change attitudes and organizations that keep people in poverty and captivity.

Popes have encouraged artists and architects to create many of the world's masterpieces: beautiful paintings of religious scenes, the great cathedrals of Europe, and countless musical compositions.

Popes have also promoted learning and the expansion of human knowledge, such as astronomy. (The Vatican Observatory, shown below, is one of the oldest astronomical research facilities in the world.) They also supported education through schools, colleges and universities.

Perhaps the greatest contribution that popes have made is their spiritual leadership of the people of God. In prayer and worship, they have led millions to a deeper relationship with God. Through their words and example, the popes teach wisdom and compassion to a world that sorely needs these gifts. In trying times, we often turn to the pope and our bishops to learn about spiritual ways we can deal with crises that threaten us.

- There are over 125,000 Catholic schools and over 5,800 Catholic hospitals in the world.

- Early forms of the Vatican Observatory have been exploring the stars since 1774. In the 1930s, the Observatory was moved to Castel Gandolfo, the pope's summer residence, about 25 kilometres southeast of Rome. In the 1960s, the Vatican moved its observatory to Arizona, in the United States, to find clear skies unaffected by city lights.

- Recent popes have spoken out about our need for conversion in how we treat the earth, so that continued life on earth is possible. They teach that people have been given the responsibility for caring for God's creation and must live up to that responsibility.

7

What qualifications do you need to be pope?

Pope John XXIII once said, "Anyone can become pope. The proof of this is that I have become one!" But it's not quite that simple.

The pope remains the pope until he dies. After his funeral, all the *cardinals* from around the world gather to elect the new pope. Imagine that you are a cardinal in the *Sistine Chapel* trying to decide who should be the next pope. You'll want to find someone who has shown good leadership, is deeply committed to the Church, and is able to establish good relations with colleagues and those outside the Church. Good luck with your choice – that description fits most of the cardinals present! That is why cardinals pray for God's guidance in this difficult decision.

While technically any male member of the Church can be elected pope, only cardinals have been elected since 1378. So how do you become a cardinal? A cardinal is a *bishop* with special responsibilities (including electing a pope). A bishop is a priest who has been chosen to oversee a local area called a *diocese*. (It is called an *archdiocese* in major centres with a large number of Catholics.) So in practice, you first need to become a priest in order to be eligible to be pope.

- There are over 130 cardinals and over 5,000 bishops in the Catholic Church. Find your diocese's website to learn more about your bishop.
- Cardinals wear special red clothing to set them apart.

8

How are popes chosen?

After a pope dies, all the cardinals in the world who are under the age of 80 gather at the *Vatican* for a special meeting called a *conclave*. This conclave of about 135 cardinals meets in the *Sistine Chapel* to elect a pope who is usually from among their group.

Each cardinal votes for a cardinal by writing the person's name on a piece of paper. The papers are placed in a chalice and counted. If more than two thirds of those present vote for one cardinal, they have elected a pope. If not, the cardinals pray and discuss among themselves and then vote again. This process continues until a pope is elected. If a two-thirds majority cannot be reached after several rounds of voting, the cardinals can decide to elect the pope with the most votes, as long as over 50 percent of them have voted for that person.

After each round of voting, the paper is stitched together and burned in a fireplace whose chimney is visible in St. Peter's Square, outside St. Peter's Basilica. This produces grey smoke, which tells the gathered crowds that another round of voting will take place. Once the cardinals have elected the pope, they add a chemical to the burning papers that turns the smoke white, and church bells are rung.

An announcement proclaims, "We have a pope!" Then, wearing a white robe called a *cassock*, the new pope is presented from an upper window to those gathered in St. Peter's Square and to millions watching online or on TV around the world. The pope then tells everyone the name he has chosen for himself. A few days later, he is officially installed in a solemn and beautiful ceremony in St. Peter's Basilica or in St. Peter's Square.

When cardinals go into the conclave, they are not allowed to communicate with the outside world, not even by cell phone. If the election takes more than one day, they sleep in recently built apartments near the Sistine Chapel. Before these were built, the cardinals slept in alcoves and broom closets!

There have been 217 popes from Italy, 17 from France, 13 from Greece, eight from Germany, three from Spain, three from Africa, and one each from Palestine, England, Portugal, the Netherlands, Switzerland and Poland.

9

How do popes get their names?

Since the year 533, popes leave behind the names they were given when they were born and adopt a new name. For example, Cardinal Josef Ratzinger became Pope Benedict XVI. This name change shows that they hold an important and distinguished position. Another way of showing their connection with tradition is the use of Roman numerals after their name. If there was an earlier pope with the same name, then the new pope adds another number to his own name. After Pope John Paul I died, Cardinal Karol Wojtyla chose the name Pope John Paul II.

Popes select their names for many different reasons. Some name themselves after biblical figures, as Pope Paul did. Some choose the name of a famous saint, as Pope Benedict did. Some choose the name of a previous pope because they want to follow in his footsteps. Pope John Paul I named himself after the two popes who reigned before him: Pope John XXIII and Pope Paul VI.

- The most commonly chosen pope names are John (23), Benedict (16), Gregory (16), Clement (14), Innocent (13), Pius (12), Leo (12) and Stephen (10).
- In 533, a Roman called Mercurius was elected pope. Because he was named after the Roman god Mercury, he changed his name to John and became Pope John II.

10

Why does the pope often wear special clothes?

In the 2 000-year history of the papacy, many symbols have been used. It is hard to know where to begin! Let's start with what the pope wears. Even if you didn't know what the pope looked like, chances are you would recognize him because his clothes are so distinctive. The pope usually wears a long, white robe called a *cassock*. Cassocks come from ancient Roman clothing called tunics. They may not make a fashion statement, but they do say that the wearers are clergy.

The pope also wears a white skullcap called a *zucchetto*. (A bishop also wears a zucchetto, but it is violet.) Many Muslims and Jews wear a skullcap for worship. To some people, it is a sign of humility before God to keep one's head covered. Other people trace it back to the headdress worn by Jewish priests and the turbans worn by other religious leaders. For them, it symbolizes the importance of the role of religious leader. This is also thought to be the origin of the tall, pointed bishop's hat called a *mitre*.

Around his neck the pope wears a Y-shaped woollen scarf called a *pallium*. There are two traditions about the origin of the pallium. One goes back to Jesus, who told us that his yoke is easy. (A yoke is something that is put across the shoulders of an animal to pull a plow or other heavy object.) Jesus meant that following his ways is not difficult. The other tradition reminds us that the wool of the pallium comes from sheep, and refers to the lost sheep that Jesus brought home safely. This meaning emphasizes the role of the pope as a shepherd to the people. Archbishops also wear the pallium, to show that they share in the teaching, ruling and sanctifying role of the pope.

When the pope begins his reign, he is given the *Fisherman's Ring*. This ring is a sign of the pope's connection with St. Peter, who fished the waters of the Sea of Galilee. The pope follows in the footsteps of St, Peter, the first leader of the Church after Jesus died. To show their love for the pope and the papacy, people sometimes kneel before the pope and kiss this ring.

Until recent years, popes have been crowned with a three-layered tiara. Starting with Pope John Paul I, new popes have chosen not to use this form of crown when they begin their service to the Church.

The pope even has special red shoes, a tradition handed down for four centuries, when red was the main colour of papal clothing rather than white.

11

Why does the pope have his own flag?

The symbolism of this flag shows how the pope is closely linked to Church traditions. The yellow and white colours are thought to relate to a symbol in the coat of arms: the keys. These keys are made of the precious metals, silver and gold. (White is used instead of silver because it is easier to reproduce white on flags.) The keys refer to a passage from Scripture where Jesus told St. Peter, the first pope, "I will give you the keys to the kingdom of heaven …." This passage gives Peter the authority to guide the Church as it tries to bring about God's kingdom on earth. A red cord joins the keys together.

The flag also includes the three-layered papal tiara, which is a type of crown. The three layers have many meanings. One possible meaning is that the pope has influence over people, the Church and heaven.

12

Where does the pope live?

The pope lives in the Vatican, in Italy. The Vatican is more than just a city; it is a small country with its own government. The pope is the head of government there. The most recognizable part of the Vatican is St. Peter's Basilica. This is the largest Christian church in the world. It was built about 500 years ago on what Christians believe is the tomb of St. Peter. Many popes are also buried near his tomb in the lower part of the church, called the crypt.

In the Vatican (shown on the next page) you can also find offices, museums and beautiful gardens. The pope has a special apartment overlooking St. Peter's Square. The apartment contains a simple bedroom, living room and office. His secretary and other assistants work in this area as well.

St. Peter's is known for its art and architecture. Michelangelo's famous sculpture, *La Pièta*, stands near the main doors. The sculpture portrays Mary's suffering as she receives the crucified body of Jesus into her arms. Near St. Peter's you can find another of Michelangelo's works: the ceiling of the *Sistine Chapel*. In this chapel, Michelangelo's paintings show many scenes from the Bible, including God's outstretched hand reaching towards Adam.

- The Vatican has its own railway station, astronomical observatory and postage stamps.
- Vatican City, which is entirely within the City of Rome, has a population of 760 people.
- The Swiss Guard is the official police force of Vatican City. If you go there, you can see some of them on official guard duty in their bright blue, red, orange and yellow uniforms.

13

What does the pope do during a normal day?

Many popes, including Pope Benedict XVI, take office when they are 70 years old or more. This is an age when most people retire, but popes don't have this luxury. In fact, they have more responsibility as pope than they ever had before.

The pope prays several times a day. He also celebrates Mass at least once a day. He prays for all the needs of the world, as well as his special intentions for the month. You can join the pope in praying these two intentions by looking them up online.

As leader of a small country, the pope often meets with foreign leaders. He tries to influence other world leaders to seek peace, justice, human rights and responsibilities, and to ensure the safety of the Church.

The pope often meets with visiting bishops and *cardinals* to hear what is going on in their local areas. He also consults them about looking after the people of their diocese and in the universal Church. The pope hosts a gathering called a papal audience for those who wish to see him and pray with him.

The pope also meets with his advisors to deal with issues that come up and to make plans. This work might include ways of improving the Church, planning for visits to other countries or appointing new bishops. The pope also writes letters to individuals, to groups of bishops and to the whole Church.

This may be a typical day for the pope, but many days contain different events as well. For example, the pope may be travelling to an area in Rome – he is the Bishop of Rome, after all! He may be going to another part of Italy or to another country. Although the pope has many responsibilities, he weaves prayer and meditation into his day. In this way, he brings the sacred into his work.

- If you went to a papal audience, you would go to a building that can hold up to 7 000 people. The pope would enter the room, greet the people, share a few words and pray with those attending. This usually happens on Wednesdays.
- Before his final illness, one of Pope John Paul II's favourite leisure activities was hiking in the Alps.
- Pope Benedict XVI spends a little time almost every day walking through the Vatican gardens.

14

Who helps the pope in his work?

You can't lead 1.3 billion people without a great deal of help. In one sense, all of God's people work with the pope. We listen to his teachings and pray for his intentions. The faithful gather in local parishes to worship and serve, guided by the teachings of the pope and the other bishops.

After Jesus died, rose again, and ascended into heaven, the *apostles* continued his work on earth. After the apostles died, other leaders, called *bishops*, carried on their work. After these bishops died, other bishops took their place. In this way we can see that the bishop in our area is connected to the apostles. Over 5 000 bishops around the world, together with the pope, offer spiritual leadership in local areas called *dioceses*.

In some of the largest communities, the bishop may be a cardinal. Cardinals are influential advisors of the pope who help to elect a new pope when the pope dies. Many cardinals lead working groups that support the pope's work.

Other advisors also help the pope do the administrative work of the *Vatican*. Whether they are clergy or lay people (non-clergy), they all have important duties in keeping the spiritual, financial and organizational life of the Church healthy.

The word *cardinal* is thought to come from the Latin word *cardinalis*, meaning "hinge" or "joint." Cardinals are important links between the pope and the rest of the Church.

The offices that support the pope's work in the Vatican are called the *curia*. Here are the main departments of the curia:

- The Secretariat of State, which looks after relations with other governments;
- The Congregation for the Doctrine of the Faith, which deals with questions about beliefs;
- The Congregation for the Causes of Saints, which oversees the process of recognizing saints;
- The Congregation for Catholic Education, which looks after Catholic schools and the training of religious (priests, monks, nuns, brothers and deacons); and
- The Congregation for Bishops, which serves the needs of bishops around the world.

15

Why does the pope travel to other countries?

Catholics from every part of the world look to the pope for leadership and inspiration. From time to time, the pope will travel to distant parts of the world to visit the faithful and their bishops and priests. Before he even says a word, the pope's presence tells the people of that land that they are important members of the Church.

The pope does much more than show up and wave to the crowds. He meets with Catholic and non-Catholic leaders to discuss important issues. For example, the pope might talk to local political leaders about human rights issues, such as how child workers are treated. With bishops, the pope might talk about ways of praying with members of other religions. Sometimes the pope meets with members and leaders of other faiths. In a trip to the Holy Land, Pope Benedict XVI met with Jewish and Muslim leaders to discuss paths to peace and deeper understanding between Christians, Muslims and Jews.

On these journeys, the pope celebrates Mass at cathedrals or in large outdoor spaces with thousands of people. He travels in a specially designed car, affectionately called the

"Popemobile." This car is designed so that he can see the people and they can see him.

- Pope John Paul II visited 129 countries when he was pope. It's not surprising that he travelled to Poland more than to any other country – he was born there!

- Pope John Paul II travelled 1,163,865 kilometres in his 102 journeys.

16

Why does the pope sometimes speak in Latin?

Jesus spoke a language called Aramaic. He could also read Hebrew, the language of the Scriptures. As soon as followers of Jesus spread his message beyond the shores of Palestine, they had to translate the message into other languages. Most people in the areas around Palestine spoke Greek. Soon the followers of Jesus wrote down the Gospels, letters and other holy books in Greek.

As Christianity spread west into the heart of the Roman Empire, followers there wanted to be able to learn and worship in their own language.

Latin was the language of the Roman Empire, and soon became the official language of worship of the Western Church. St. Jerome translated the Bible from Hebrew and Greek into Latin. As the Bishop of Rome, the pope was recognized as the leader of the Western Church, so he would speak in Latin.

By the time the Roman Empire ended, Western Christianity was established in Europe, West Asia and North Africa. Many areas had their own language, but priests and monks used Latin to communicate with each other. There was another important reason to keep Latin as the official language. At a time when the Church no longer had the protection of the Roman army, Christians needed to stick together. Worshipping together in Latin was an important symbol of unity in a time of great distress.

Until the 1960s, the prayers of the Mass were in Latin. At the *Second Vatican Council*, the bishops decided that it was more important for people to understand the Mass in their own language than to keep Latin as a symbol of unity and tradition. This change helped worshippers to focus on Jesus Christ as the proper sign of unity for Christians.

There are times in worship when it is good to emphasize the tradition and unity of the Church. At such times, you may hear Latin spoken. For example, the priest may say *Agnus dei* instead of "Lamb of God." The pope uses Latin when he doesn't want to show a preference for any particular language. His official letters, called *encyclicals*, are written in Latin to show that they are important messages for the whole Church. The letters are then translated into many languages so more people can understand them.

Every day, you speak words that come from Latin: ridiculous, necessary, library, relevant, message, humble, diary, reptile, strict and (of course) religion. Many English and French (and Spanish, Italian and Portuguese) words come from Latin.

When a new pope is announced to the world, the Latin words "*Habemus Papam!*" are spoken. This means "We have a pope."

17

Why does the pope make rules for Catholics?

Have you ever tried to play a game without knowing the rules? Chances are that it didn't last very long. Chaos usually breaks out when the rules aren't clear. When humans do things that are complicated, it is best to follow the wisdom of those who have done those things before or to follow the rules laid out for a system. Life is about as complicated as it gets. People hurt each other without even meaning to. So all cultures have rules to make things easier. For example, almost all cultures agree that you shouldn't deliberately hurt someone else or steal from them.

Christians found helpful rules for living in the wisdom of the Jewish people and especially in the teachings and example of Jesus Christ. The Church carried on in the footsteps of Jesus and the *apostles* by applying Christian ideas to new situations, such as nuclear war.

As new issues arise, such as creating artificial life, global warming and Internet communications, the teachings of Jesus need to be interpreted again and again. The pope works with bishops and experts to write formal statements on these topics. These statements contain rules to help people live holy lives in difficult times. These decisions are made after long periods of prayer and research. Sometimes people get impatient with the Church and want teachings changed to match what is popular and easy. But the pope cannot ignore the teachings of the Gospel, and so he seeks the guidance of the Holy Spirit through prayer.

- *Canon law* lists all the official rules of the Church. (A canon is a complete list.)

- Another place where the teachings and explanations for many of these laws are found is in a book called the *Catechism of the Catholic Church*.

18

How does the pope show his special love for young people?

In 1984, Pope John Paul II hosted the first World Youth Day in Rome. Young people from around the world came together at this special festival to worship, celebrate and serve together. This event is now held every two or three years, in a different country each time, and lasts for several days. World Youth Days have been held in Argentina, Australia, Canada, Germany, the Philippines, Poland, Spain and the United States.

The host country prepares by setting up huge outdoor facilities for gatherings and planning the procession of the World Youth Day Cross from place to place. The youth visitors, called pilgrims, often arrive before the events begin. They stay in dioceses around the country, doing acts of service, prayer and worship. The opening festivities often include celebrations and prayer services marked by great joy. The pope usually joins in these events, celebrating Mass and taking part in the Stations of the Cross. The grand finale is an overnight vigil where everyone sleeps under the stars and hundreds of thousands of people celebrate the final Mass together. The Mass is also broadcast on TV and online so people can watch all over the globe.

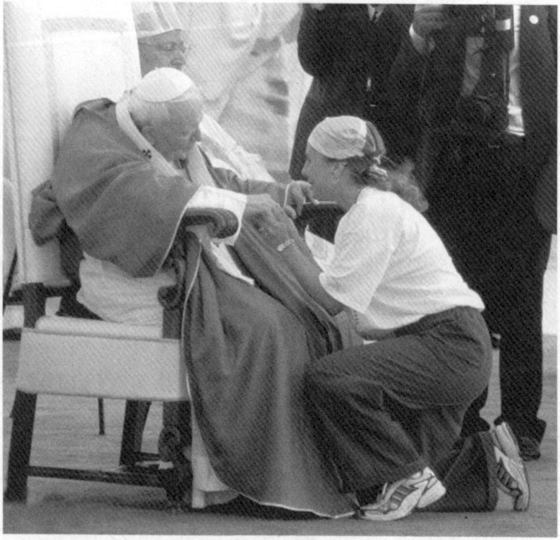

Recent popes have also reached out to young people by investing energy and time in Catholic schools. Pope John Paul II issued this challenge in Manila at the 1995 World Youth Day: "Are you capable of giving yourselves, your time, your energy and your talent to the well-being of others? Are you capable of love? If you are, Church and society can expect great things of each one of you."

- The largest World Youth Day Mass was held in Manila in 1995. Five million people attended! This is the largest Mass on record.

- Here are the dates and locations of some recent World Youth Days: Rome 2000, Toronto 2002, Cologne 2005, Sydney 2008, Madrid 2011.

- In years when there is no international gathering, World Youth Day is celebrated around the world on Passion (Palm) Sunday. The pope gives a special message for youth on that day.

- Each World Youth Day has a theme taken from scripture. Madrid chose the theme "Rooted and built up in Jesus Christ, firm in the faith" (Colossians 2:7).

19

How can we help the pope in his work?

Catholics see the pope and the bishops as following in the footsteps of the *apostles*. Jesus called upon the disciples to continue the work of teaching the Good News and healing people physically and spiritually. We can work with the pope in many ways to help the world become a more loving, just and prayerful place. To do this, we must develop some good habits.

In our homes, we are not only to use kind words, but also to do kind deeds. The pope calls us to serve each other as brothers and sisters. At home you can serve your siblings and your parents by doing at least one kind thing each day that is not expected of you. This habit of kindness serves others, but it will also make your life brighter. You will know that you can make a difference in other people's lives.

One of the important tasks for young people is to learn about our Christian story and our Catholic teachings. You may get some of this information from your family, your Catholic school or your parish. There's a lot of good information on the Internet, but make sure the site is reliable. You can find the Vatican on Facebook and on other social media sites. Develop the habit of curiosity about the Catholic faith by asking and answering one key question a day.

The pope is a very busy man with great responsibilities, yet he finds time several times a day to pray. Prayer is a way of opening our hearts and minds to God. We can pray familiar prayers such as the Our Father, we can pray to God using our own words, or we can pray by listening for how God is speaking to us. We might hear God in the words of the Bible, in the advice of wise people, or in the beauty of creation. Catholics believe that we connect with God most deeply through the Mass, so this is another place to pray. If we take time to pray daily, this good habit will bring us alongside the pope in making this world a more sacred place.

- A prayer attributed to St. Teresa of Avila asks us to be the hands, feet and eyes of Christ on this earth. How is this possible?
- To find the social media sites that the Vatican uses, go to www.pope2you.net/.
- Praying at the kitchen table is a great way to bring your family together. Say or sing grace before meals together, or pray the Our Father, the Hail Mary or the Rosary as a family.

??????????? 20 ???????????

Why doesn't the pope sell all the treasures of the Church to help poor people?

Enemies of the pope and the Church often accuse the *Vatican* of hoarding millions of dollars while poor people starve. This view is based on the belief that the Church has vast resources in its artwork and treasures that it could easily sell. Yet many of the riches of the Church are a gift of beauty to the world found in art and in sacred buildings. The Church must legally and morally preserve them for future generations. While the Church in the past may have had the money to build beautiful cathedrals and buy art, it does not have extra money for these projects today.

The pope does not own anything – not even a home or a car. He doesn't need anything like that. He has responsibility for how the Church spends its money, but the days when popes made money from their papal office are long gone. His life is devoted to serving God, God's people and God's creation. That is not to say that he has no personal pleasures. Pope Benedict XVI, for example, loves to play classical music on the piano or take a holiday in the northern Italian mountains.

The Church is a large organization that is responsible for over a billion people throughout the world. The Church needs to manage its resources carefully to help people now and in the future. Today, the Church is the largest source of charitable support in the world. Twenty-five percent of the financial support worldwide for people with HIV/AIDS comes from Catholic churches or organizations, including health care and educational institutions that different Church groups have set up.

- Catholic teaching tells us that we must have "a preferential option for the poor." That means that we should take special care of them, as Jesus did.

- Catholics have important ways of supporting the poor through aid groups including Development and Peace (Canada), Catholic Relief Services (United States), CAFOD (United Kingdom) and Caritas (many countries).

21

Why is the pope always a man?

According to the New Testament, all of the *apostles* whom Jesus left behind to continue his work were men. The pope and the bishops trace their leadership roles directly back to these apostles. In the early days of the Church, many of the popes were deacons. As the role of the priest and bishop became defined, the Bishop of Rome was accepted as pope. So there has been a long tradition of having only males as deacons, priests, bishops, cardinals and popes.

This does not mean that there is no role for women in the Church. In recent years, the Church has canonized (recognized as saints) as many women as men. It has spoken out for equal rights for women in the workforce, in politics and in other areas of society.

- There was a rumour that a woman (Joan) actually ruled as Pope John during the Middle Ages. Her disguise is supposed to have failed when she gave birth! Most historians do not believe that this story is true.

- Women have had important roles in Church history. Mary, the mother of Jesus, was chosen to bear God's son. St. Teresa of Avila and St. Theresa of Lisieux are Doctors of the Church because of their contributions to theology. One of the most beloved and influential Catholics of recent years is Blessed Mother Teresa of Calcutta, who cared for the poor and dying in India and saw her work spread around the world.

22

What happens if the pope makes a mistake?

All popes make mistakes, because they are human. Sometimes they will make little mistakes because of forgetfulness or accidents. This is understandable. If the pope has spiritual difficulties, he uses the Sacrament of Reconciliation to heal wounded relationships with God and others.

In serious matters of teaching the faith, however, popes rarely make mistakes. Before making important decisions, the pope asks cardinals, bishops and other experts for advice. He also spends a lot of time in prayer to make sure his decisions are pleasing to God. The pope may speak infallibly (free of the possibility of error) on a matter of faith. This has happened only once since the Church stated in 1870 that the pope can teach infallibly: in 1950, Pope Pius XII declared that the body and soul of Jesus' mother, the Blessed Virgin Mary, were taken up into heaven at the end of her life on earth. Many also believe that Pope Pius IX's statement that Mary was born without sin (the Immaculate Conception) is also an infallible statement.

Years ago there were some popes who did not lead holy lives. In fact, some of them were villains. The faithful reacted against such abuses by ensuring that the popes who followed were men of virtue and deep faith. Still, the Church has made mistakes. In recent years, popes have apologized for things that happened many years earlier. For example, Pope John Paul II apologized for how the Church treated Galileo, a scientist who insisted that the Earth revolved around the sun (at the time, this finding went against how the Church saw the world). As time passed, it became clear that the Church was mistaken because it did not yet know all the scientific facts. Although the pope is deeply connected to God, he is human and can make mistakes.

A number of popes have apologized for the Church's past mistakes:

- Pope John Paul II apologized to the people of West Africa for Christian participation in the slave trade.
- In the Jubilee Year of 2000, Pope John Paul II apologized for Church wrongs that were done towards women, Jews and minorities.
- Pope Benedict XVI apologized to young people who were abused by priests.

The Church is constantly learning and growing in faith and trying to do God's will. Many Catholics pray for the Church so that its actions help people grow closer to God and share God's love with all people.

23

What happens when popes come into conflict with political leaders?

After the Catholic Church guided Western Europe through the turbulent centuries following the fall of the Roman Empire, kingdoms and empires emerged to take political control over much of Europe. At times, politicians and popes came into conflict. Here are two examples of popes who struggled with politicians to protect Church interests.

The dark ages of social chaos were replaced by a more organized political system. In Western Europe, the Holy Roman Emperor challenged the authority of the Church. The Emperor saw himself as the political ruler of Europe. Pope Innocent III, a pope in the thirteenth century, accepted this point of view as long as the Emperor accepted Innocent as God's representative on Earth and reported to him. Innocent used his power to lay out moral laws that all Catholics were called to obey, and to set standards for how all people should worship.

If you had lived 500 years ago, it would have been hard to say that the pope was a good and wise man. Julius II was an example of a pope who used his political power in ways that didn't follow the example of Jesus and the *apostles*. Julius was more of a warrior than a spiritual leader. He felt at home in a suit of armour. He was also a great supporter of the arts.

Under the direction of Julius, the painter Michelangelo completed the famous ceiling of the *Sistine Chapel* in the Vatican, which you can still visit today. Popes who had difficulty being spiritual leaders were one of the reasons why many people left the Church during the Protestant Reformation a few years later. (For more about the Reformation, see *25 Questions about Founders of the World's Major Religions.*) The Catholic Church set higher standards after this difficult time, with more of a focus on spiritual leadership.

In 1054, the Eastern Orthodox Church broke away from the Western Church and refused to recognize the pope as the leader of Christianity. Recently, the pope and Orthodox leaders have been holding talks about healing these wounds.

Between the years 1000 and 1500, the Church built beautiful cathedral churches that are still standing today. It also helped to found universities in Italy (Padua and Bologna), France (Paris) and England (Oxford and Cambridge).

24

How can popes help the poor?

Many popes followed the command of Jesus to take special care of the poor. Pope Leo XIII was one of them. Just over a hundred years ago, working and living conditions in many towns and cities were very harsh. Many people worked long hours in dangerous conditions for low wages. Pope Leo called for changes to a way of thinking that allowed people to be treated in such an undignified way. He wrote about this in a letter called *Rerum Novarum*, which is Latin for "New Things." (Papal documents are often known by their Latin names, which are taken from the first few words of the text.) This letter marked a shift in Church policy: from this point on, the Church started to comment more strongly on social issues. For many years, the Church had supported schools, hospitals, orphanages and aid for the poor. This letter, however, went further, questioning the causes of injustice instead of just working with victims of injustice.

Since Leo's time, popes have spoken out against war, abortion, poverty, pollution and many other harmful actions. Organizations such as the St. Vincent de Paul Society, Missionaries of Charity and Catholic pro-life groups have been inspired and encouraged by the popes' support for social justice.

In the early 1200s, St. Francis of Assisi was working with the poor and diseased. In many ways, St. Francis is a model for 21st-century Christians, especially in his outreach to Muslims and his concern for ecology.

Leo XIII was the first pope whose voice was recorded. He was also the first pope to be filmed on the motion picture camera.

25

Can the Church change?

When Pope John XXIII started his papacy in 1958 at the age of 76, many expected him to have a short reign and not make a significant mark in the Church. How wrong they were! Although he was pope for only five years before he died, "Good Pope John," as people called him, changed the face of the Catholic Church. He wanted to "open the windows" of the Church to let in fresh ideas, so from 1962 to 1965 he gathered all the bishops at a series of meetings called the *Second Vatican Council*, or *Vatican II*. (These meetings are named after the city where they are held. This was the second such council to be held at the Vatican. The first was in 1869 to 1870.) Pope John wanted to make the Church more influential in the modern world, but at the same time he wanted to return to the energy and passion of the early Church in spreading the Good News of God's love for all people.

Although he did not live to see the end of the council, his influence was felt as changes in the Church began to be put in place. Here are some of these changes:

- Priests could celebrate Mass in the language of the worshippers (before this time, the Mass prayers were all in Latin, which was no longer a spoken language);

- The idea that the Church was a community of God's people was emphasized more;
- Dialogue with other religions, science and other aspects of culture was encouraged;
- Action to support the poor and oppressed was promoted.

The conditions of our world changed greatly during the last hundred years. It had suffered through two world wars, a huge shift in population from the country to the cities, and a rapid growth in technology. Pope John XXIII saw that the Holy Spirit was calling for the Church to respond in new ways to these changes. He had the courage to lead the Church forward into the modern world. In the year 2000, this holy man received the title "Blessed." This is one of the steps towards recognizing him as a saint.

During the Second World War, the future Pope John XXIII served as a diplomat. He helped thousands of Jews escape death in the Nazi concentration camps.

Over 3 000 bishops and other experts took part in Vatican II.

Pope Paul VI, who was crowned in 1963, followed Pope John XXIII.

WORDS TO KNOW

Apostle: A person who spread the message of Jesus in the first century.

Archbishop: A bishop who is responsible for a large diocese.

Archdiocese: An area with a large number of Catholics, priests and churches.

Bishop: A priest who is chosen and ordained to oversee a group of people, their clergy and their parishes in a specific area.

Canon Law: The official set of Church laws.

Cardinal: A bishop or archbishop who has special responsibilities, including choosing a new pope.

Cassock: Long robes worn by a priest.

Catacombs: The caverns and burial places in Rome where early Christians gathered for worship.

Conclave: The gathering of cardinals to elect a new pope.

Curia: The different offices or departments of the Vatican.

Diocese: An area overseen by a bishop.

Encyclical: An official letter that the pope sends to the Church.

Fisherman's Ring: The ring the pope wears that shows that he follows in the footsteps of St. Peter.

Mitre: The tall, pointed hat that the pope and bishops wear.

Monastery: A place where monks or nuns live lives devoted to seeking God through prayer and service.

Pallium: A narrow, Y-shaped scarf that popes and archbishops wear.

Pontiff: An ancient title of the supreme priest of Rome, inherited from the ancient Romans.

Primate: The leader of a Church in a country.

Second Vatican Council: A meeting called by Pope John XXIII. The goal of this meeting was to bring together all the bishops to provide a renewed vision for how the Church should continue its mission. It was also called Vatican II.

Sistine Chapel: The chapel in the Vatican where papal elections take place. The ceiling was painted by Michelangelo nearly 500 years ago.

Vatican: The 44-hectare section of Rome that is actually a small country. It is the headquarters of the Roman Catholic Church, home of the pope and home of St. Peter's Basilica.

Vatican II: *See* Second Vatican Council.

Zucchetto: The small skullcap worn by bishops, cardinals and the pope. The pope's zucchetto is usually white.

TIMELINE C

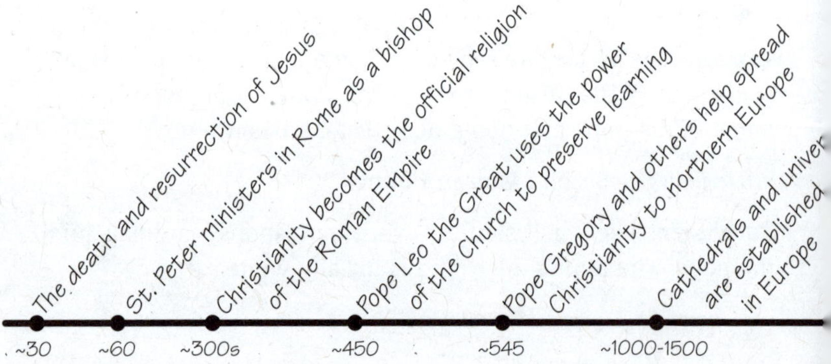

*** All years are AD (Anno Domini, or Year of the Lord). These are the years after the birth of Jesus. (The sign " ~ " means "approximately," because these dates are not exact.)**

HURCH HISTORY

nocent III reinforces the Church politically and morally.

St. Francis of Assisi ministers to the poor and sick in Italy.

0

The reign of Pope Julius II, and the Protestant Reformation

~1500-1530

Pope Leo XIII writes about social justice

late 1800s

Pope John XXIII opens the Second Vatican Council to bring changes to the Catholic Church

1962-1965

The reign of Pope John Paul II

1978-2005

Benedict XVI is elected pope

2005